ADOLESCENT RIGHTS

Are Young People Equal Under the Law?

Keith Greenberg

Twenty-First Century Books

A Division of Henry Holt and Company
New York

Twenty-First Century Books
A division of Henry Holt and Company, Inc.
115 West 18th Street
New York, New York 10011

Henry Holt® and colophon are registered trademarks of Henry Holt and Company, Inc.
Publishers since 1866

©1995 by Blackbirch Graphics, Inc.
First Edition
5 4 3 2 1
All rights reserved.
No part of this book may be reproduced in any form without permission in writing from the publisher, except by a reviewer.

Published in Canada by Fitzhenry & Whiteside Ltd.
195 Allstate Parkway, Markham, Ontario L3R 4T8

Printed in the United States of America

Created and produced in association with Blackbirch Graphics, Inc.

Library of Congress Cataloging-in-Publication Data

Greenberg, Keith Elliot.
    Adolescent rights: are young people equal under the law?/Keith Greenberg.
      p.   cm. — (Issues of our time)
    Includes bibliographical references and index.
    Summary: Provides an overview of how the legal system has treated children in the past and discusses the rights young people have today.
    ISBN 0-8050-3877-9 (acid-free paper)
    1. Teenagers—Legal status, laws, etc.—United States—Juvenile literature. 2. Children's rights—United States—Juvenile literature. 3. Minors—United States—Juvenile literature. [1. Teenagers—Legal status, laws, etc. 2. Children's rights. 3. Law.] I. Title. II. Series.
KF479.Z9G7   1995
346.7301'35—dc20
[347.306135]
                                                                           94-41753
                                                                               CIP
                                                                                AC

Contents

1. A Vital Topic — 5
2. Going to Court — 15
3. Children's Rights in School — 27
4. Problems at Home — 41
5. Looking Ahead — 53

Glossary — 60

For Further Reading — 61

Source Notes — 62

Index — 63

1

A Vital Topic

The case had the attention of people everywhere. Could a twelve-year-old boy "divorce" his mother? It was happening in Florida, in 1992, where Gregory Kingsley was fighting to cut ties with the woman he said neglected him.

Child advocates—adults who speak out for children's rights—called the case a landmark. They stated that, under certain conditions, children should be allowed to take legal action against their parents. Now, children could define what was in their own "best interests"; it was no longer a matter to be determined only by parents, legal guardians, and other adults.

But Gregory Kingsley's reason for going to court was much more personal. "I'm doing it for me so I can be happy," he said.

In 1992, in this Florida court, Gregory Kingsley asked to be legally separated from his mother, Rachel (at the witness stand, in white).

The First Child Abuse Case

American society has come a long way since the 1800s, when children were regarded as possessions like cattle and farm tools.

That started to change in 1874, when a little girl named Mary Ellen McCormack entered a New York courtroom and told a horrifying tale of abuse.

"I don't know how old I am," she said. "I have never had but one pair of shoes. . . . My bed at night is only a piece of carpet stretched on the floor underneath a window. . . . Mamma has been in the habit of . . . beating me almost every day. I have now on my head two black-and-blue marks which were made by mamma with the whip. . . . Whenever mamma went out, I was locked up in the bedroom. . . . I have no recollection of ever being in the street in my life."

Mary Ellen's father had been killed in the Civil War, and her mother had not been able to support her. She was adopted by Thomas and Mary McCormack. But after Thomas died, his wife remarried and the child was treated as a burden. She was beaten and forced to stay in a closet, deprived of daylight. Rarely was she even allowed to bathe.

A year earlier, Etta Angell Wheeler, a social worker in New York City, heard about Mary Ellen from a neighbor. Since the laws forbade outsiders to intrude upon what went on in a child's home,

Wheeler took a creative approach. She contacted Henry Bergh, founder of the American Society for the Prevention of Cruelty to Animals. Since Mary Ellen was a member of the animal kingdom, she argued, Bergh should assist the child. He agreed.

Mary Ellen's adoptive mother was charged with assault with intent to kill. More importantly, the children's rights movement was formed. A major leader of this movement was Bergh's attorney, Elbridge Gerry, who spent much of his life protecting the rights of children. On December 15, 1874, Gerry, Bergh, and others founded the New York Society for the Prevention of Cruelty to Children.

Elbridge Gerry was the president of the New York Society for the Prevention of Cruelty to Children for forty years.

Important Laws

Still, it took more than sixty-five years for the first significant decision regarding the rights of children. In 1941, the Supreme Court—the nation's highest court—upheld a child-labor law Congress had passed in 1938. This ban on child labor ended nearly forty years of children working in factories for long hours and under miserable conditions.

Another decision came in 1943, when the Supreme Court ruled that students who are Jehovah's Witnesses—whose faith prohibits saluting a flag of any country—and others with similar beliefs, have a constitutional right to refuse to participate in the Pledge of Allegiance.

ADOLESCENT RIGHTS

Does America Really Believe in Children's Rights?

Observers of the American justice system have sometimes complained that youngsters have "too much freedom" in America. After all, the United States is where children have challenged the authority of both their parents and school in the courtroom.

But, despite this activity, others believe the U.S. government has not done its share to help children when compared with an international level. "The policy of the United States toward children has been very backward," said Nina Meyerhof, who coordinates programs promoting international children's rights. In 1990, when a special conference included the Convention on the Rights of the Child, she pointed out the United States was one of a handful of nations that did not endorse the measure.

"One hundred and thirty countries have signed it," she said, "twenty have not. The United States is one of the countries... along with Libya, Iraq, and South Africa. These are our bedfellows."

When Representative Bernie Sanders of Vermont introduced a resolution in Congress to support the Convention on the Rights of the Child, President George Bush did not support it. Among the reasons given: The document did not ban abortion and it called for forbidding capital punishment for anyone under the age of eighteen. Bush was against abortion rights and in favor of capital punishment.

Because President Bill Clinton and his wife, Hillary Rodham Clinton, have supported children's rights for years, Meyerhof said she hoped the Clinton administration would make an effort to support this and similar measures. And, she added, just as Americans are guaranteed freedom in the Constitution, children would gain important liberties with this new document. "With this bill of rights, children will be able to claim a role in deciding their future," Meyerhof said. "In fact, I'm more interested in the document as a tool for children than in the actual document itself."

A third important change came in 1967, when the Supreme Court first ordered that minors receive the same protection as adult defendants, including a court-appointed attorney if they needed one.

A few years later, young people won another battle. In the midst of the Vietnam War, the country was divided over whether the United States should be fighting in Southeast Asia. To show their disapproval of the conflict, many students began wearing black armbands with peace symbols to school. Some administrators objected, and the issue was taken to court. In 1969, the Supreme Court ruled that students had a right to wear the armbands as a form of symbolic speech, which is protected by free-speech provisions of the First Amendment.

But young people were still unhappy. They complained that at age eighteen they could be drafted into the military—and sent to Vietnam to risk their lives—but could not vote until they turned twenty-one. In 1970, this situation changed, when the U.S. Congress lowered the voting age to eighteen.

After that, young people could take a stand on election day. But many children still felt powerless, especially when they got tangled up in the legal system. In 1990, the Supreme Court appointed an attorney to protect a child's rights involved in a case. This was the first time the 1967 provision had been used in an abuse case.

Young People and Crime

One of the reasons so many people are concerned about children's rights is that more young people are engaging in crime than ever before. Between 1986 and 1991, murders committed by teenagers between fourteen and eighteen years old jumped an incredible 124 percent. Children of all ethnic backgrounds have gotten involved in violent crime, many times for reasons that make little, if any, sense. In California, for instance, a teenage girl was killed by two friends because they were jealous of her hair.

There are many factors contributing to this dangerous trend. Some children come from homes disrupted by divorce, drugs, and alcohol. With parents absorbed in these complex problems, young people may be negatively influenced. Also, children who have suffered physical and sexual abuse sometimes abuse others in the same way.

Young people have little trouble obtaining drugs and weapons. A deadly combination is crack cocaine, which tends to make the user violent, and the rising number of guns available to young people. A U.S. Department of Justice report stated that 100,000

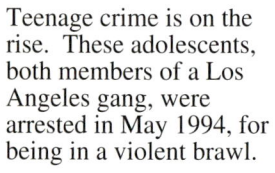

Teenage crime is on the rise. These adolescents, both members of a Los Angeles gang, were arrested in May 1994, for being in a violent brawl.

American students carry guns to school each day. Because children are likely to be more reckless than adults, triggers are often pulled over meaningless things, such as a dirty look or the theft of a pair of sneakers.

Frequently, however, authorities are lenient with teenagers who commit crimes. In their view, teens are still children and are still learning right from wrong; they are not as responsible for their actions as adults. Juvenile courts—courts that handle minors' cases—were created to be better able to deal with children. Their purpose is not as much to punish as to guide children. Judges may consult psychologists and social workers to determine which type of treatment would be most helpful for a young person.

This pistol was recovered from a student in a New York City school in March 1992, during a school board crackdown on guns.

ADOLESCENT RIGHTS 11

Certain crimes, however, like murder and rape, are so shocking that officials may choose to prosecute a teenager as an adult. That means that the young person faces the same severe penalties as an older person—long sentences, life in prison, even the death penalty. Rather than being sent to a juvenile detention facility, where the aim is frequently to rehabilitate a young person, a youth can be confined in a penitentiary with adults who are also regarded as vicious criminals.

Is this always fair? Many supporters claim that teenagers are mature enough to grasp the seriousness of their crimes. But others believe that young people often get into trouble because society has failed them.

Brian was fifteen when he was arrested for possession of cocaine in Chicago. Police believe he intended to sell the drug. In another time, Brian may have been viewed as a teenager who needed direction to straighten out his life. But people in his home state of Illinois were fed up with rising crime. If a young person didn't hesitate before breaking the law, they asked, why should society hesitate before punishing a teenager?

Brian was arrested near a schoolyard. Under a tough Illinois law, an adult court would decide the case of anyone—regardless of age—charged with drug dealing within 1,000 feet of a school. That

Youth and Crime: What's Punishment Like?

What happens to a young person who steals a car, gets arrested during a gang fight, or is picked up for selling drugs?

Often, judges send these youths to a juvenile detention facility. Some of these places look like prisons, with bars and cells. Others could be mistaken for college campuses, with cottages and well-trimmed lawns. Regardless of the appearance of the location, many of the same problems exist.

The centers are frequently overcrowded. At one facility in Virginia, a study reported that youths were forced to sleep on bathroom floors. In a Maryland facility, young people slept in recreation and laundry rooms because cells were too cramped.

Often there is violence. At the Beaumont Learning Center in Powhatan, Virginia, a teacher was raped and a supervisor beaten with a weight during two separate incidents in 1993. Fights were very common. The young people confined to the center were there for offenses as serious as rape, arson, and murder.

And Beaumont is one of the better places. Its cottages stand on rolling green hills, with no fences surrounding the facility. Administrators try to rehabilitate, rather than simply punish, the young people. But to an inmate surrounded by peers with such dangerous pasts, this can still be a very frightening place.

Administrators understand the potential for violence and do everything they can to limit it. The restrictions leave the young inmates with very little freedom. Guards follow them when they leave their cottages and search them after classes each day. Complained one teenager, "The only time I'm alone is when I'm going to the bathroom."

meant that Brian would be facing up to six years in an adult prison.

"What does a kid know at fifteen?" his father questioned. "How can you hold a kid at that age responsible for adulthood? There's got to be another way."

However, as time passes, the number of youngsters in Brian's position multiplies. The teenage crime wave has become an epidemic. As police and courts battle, increasing numbers of teenagers are asking themselves, "Just what *are* my rights?"

ADOLESCENT RIGHTS

2

Going to Court

Gregory Kingsley's biological—or natural—mother, Rachel, knew what it felt like to be deprived. Her mother died when she was nine and Rachel had to take on the responsibilities of an adult.

Years later, when her son went to court to "divorce" her, many felt sorry for Rachel. "She's had enough abuse, you know?" her father, Maxwell Sutton, said sadly when he testified.

Even Lizabeth Russ, who won custody of Gregory from Rachel, expressed sympathy for the woman. "I can't help but feel that if she had a different childhood, she'd be a different mother and this wouldn't be happening to her," Russ said.

Judge Thomas S. Kirk shakes Gregory Kingsley's hand after Gregory won his custody case. The boy's foster father, George Russ, stands behind him.

A Tough Life

Unfortunately, Rachel was not able to put her troubles behind her. She married an alcoholic. When Gregory was four and Rachel was pregnant with her third child, the couple separated.

Gregory did not know where he belonged. Once he thought he was going to stay with his father, Ralph, for a short time. Instead, father and son spent almost five years roaming around the country.

Then, in 1989, Gregory was living with his mother and brothers again. She thought she could support them, but it was impossible. After five months, Gregory was shifted to a different home. He lived with one foster—or temporary—family, then two others. Gregory wished his mother would come for him, but he did not know where she was.

Eventually, he found himself in the Lake County Boys Ranch, a home for youngsters suffering from abuse and neglect.

Meeting a New Father

Like Gregory, George Russ was the son of an alcoholic. But Russ was determined not to fall into the same pattern as his father. He worked hard and attended college, then the University of Florida Law School.

Russ became a successful lawyer, but never forgot the distress he felt as a child. When he was not working, he involved himself in activities to help young people. During a visit to the Lake County Boys Ranch in 1991, he met Gregory. While the other boys were busy playing, Gregory was sitting alone, reading a book.

Russ felt the need to do something to help Gregory. When he arrived home after his visit to the boys' home, he told his wife, Lizabeth, about the lonely child he had seen. "How is he going to turn out if he doesn't have a true family?" Russ asked. "If he doesn't have a father?"

The couple spent the night talking about the situation. As religious members of the Mormon faith, they also prayed for an answer. Finally, they decided to bring Gregory into their Orlando, Florida, home as a foster child.

Living with the Russes Gregory did not feel alone any longer—the Russes had five sons and three daughters. He seemed to appreciate the smallest gestures. When the Russes took him shopping, he was grateful to receive a lunch box with a thermos. All his life, he had wanted to have his own thermos to bring chocolate milk to school.

"He used to cling to us," Lizabeth Russ said. "I'd be in the kitchen washing dishes, and every ten minutes, he'd come, hug me for fifteen seconds, and walk away." Soon, he was calling the Russes "Dad" and "Mom." He also gave himself a new name, Shawn.

The Legal Battle

After Gregory had been with the Russes for five months, Rachel Kingsley told a state social service agency she wanted Gregory back. The agency was ready to help. Generally, the government tries to keep a child in foster care no more than eighteen months. After that, efforts are made to place the youngster in a permanent home. Sometimes the child will be adopted by another family. But much of the time, the state tries to reunite the young person with his or her parents.

When Gregory was told that his mother wanted to take him from the Russes, he became upset. George Russ claimed that the boy told him, "I will *not* go back. What can I do to stay with you?"

In September 1992, twelve-year-old Gregory went to court to change his parents. Witnesses testified that Rachel, an unemployed waitress,

Here, Gregory Kingsley is shown with his foster family, the Russes, who supported him during his legal battle.

used alcohol and drugs, and had hit her son. Rachel told the court she had given Gregory to foster care three times because she could not support him.

But Gregory told how badly he felt as he moved from one place to another, never sure when he would see Rachel again. During a period of eight years, he had lived with her for only seven months.

After he left his first foster home, Gregory said Rachel vowed they would be together forever. But he ended up in foster care twice afterward.

"I just thought she didn't care anymore," he said. "I figured that if she breaks her promise, she just doesn't care very much." Although Gregory felt sorry for her, he said "I don't love her like a mom."

On September 25, 1992, after a two-day trial, Judge Thomas S. Kirk said that there was "clear and convincing evidence" that Gregory had been "abandoned and neglected" by his mother. He ruled that Rachel no longer had the rights of a natural mother and that the Russes were now free to adopt Gregory.

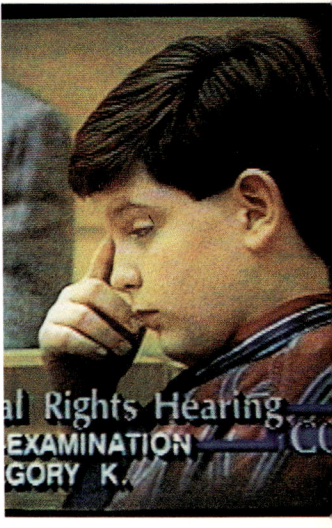

At his hearing, Gregory testified that his mother never visited, called, or wrote while he was in foster care for two years. He said, "I just thought she forgot about me."

Reaction to the Verdict

The story made headlines around the world. Legal experts said no child had ever officially "divorced" a parent before. Although the trial was over, the debate continued.

Rachel's lawyer, Jane Carey, said the decision was harmful to families. One child's wishes, she argued,

Rachel Kingsley (in white) officially lost custody of her son to the Russes in September 1992.

appeared to be more important than keeping a family together. Many wanted Gregory to win, she said, "but that has torn this family apart."

But Howard Davidson, an authority on children's rights, told the *New York Times* that the verdict had a positive impact. "The case clearly sends a message to parents that they are not free to neglect and mistreat children," he said.

Gregory—or Shawn Russ—sent a message to other children. "If a child doesn't have a good life, and they're truly not happy—and not because their parents won't buy them something—they should talk to somebody and find out if [going to court] is the right thing for them," he said in an interview in *Ladies Home Journal* magazine. "I know it was the right thing for me, to do what I did. I like it here and I'm happy. I love my new mom and dad."

The Kimberly Mays Case On December 2, 1978, Regina Twigg gave birth to a girl at Hardee Memorial Hospital in Wauchula, Florida. She and her husband,

Ernest, named the pretty, blue-eyed child Arlena Beatrice. In the delivery room, the baby seemed healthy. But two days later, the Twiggs were told that the infant had a heart ailment.

"When we were handed Arlena the second day at the hospital, I knew something was wrong," Regina said. "I'd had a six-pound, eight-ounce, very healthy-looking baby. But Arlena was unhealthy looking. She had a heartbeat that sounded like a machine—you could feel it through her back."

Regina was puzzled and asked the nurse if this was the right baby. The nurse simply pointed at the child's ID (identification) bracelet with the name "Twigg."

Arlena Twigg, shown here at about the age of eight.

The infant's condition brought back memories of another baby girl Regina Twigg had, Vivia. Three years earlier, Vivia had been born ill and died after just two months. The Twiggs wondered whether this baby had inherited a similar condition.

The Twiggs brought Arlena home and began caring for her, doing everything possible to help her. Nine days after Arlena was born, she was back in the hospital for emergency surgery. This would

ADOLESCENT RIGHTS

Robert Mays, Kimberly's father, takes questions in his attorney's office in October 1988, regarding his daughter's case.

happen again and again for the next nine years. On August 23, 1988, Arlena died after heart surgery. She was nine and a half years old.

Months earlier, Arlena had had to go through a series of examinations. When the results of one blood test came back, the Twiggs were stunned. The couple learned that the child had type B blood, but everyone else in the family was type O. They began to suspect that something had happened at the hospital and they got the wrong child by mistake.

The Twiggs examined Arlena's birth certificate. They were shocked to see that she had at first been described as a healthy child. Later, someone had added a notation stating that Arlena suffered from heart disease. Convinced that their real baby had been switched with another child, they investigated public records. The information soon led them to a girl in Sarasota, Florida, named Kimberly Michelle Mays. Like Arlena, she had blond hair and blue eyes. The two were the only white babies born at Hardee Memorial Hospital the same week.

Kimberly's parents, Robert and Barbara, had their daughter on November 29, 1978. But Barbara died of cancer two years later. As Kimberly grew up, she and her father became very close. Robert had re-married, but the marriage ended in divorce. When the Twiggs tracked her down, Kimberly and her father were the only ones living in their house.

Kimberly was asked to undergo several tests to determine if she was indeed the Twiggs' child. On the day the results came back, Robert asked Kimberly to sit in the living room because he had to tell her something important. "Am I your daughter?" Kimberly asked. "Oh, yes, you're my daughter," he answered. Kimberly broke into a smile before Robert added, "but unfortunately, you're not my biological daughter."

Kimberly jumped into Robert's arms, crying. Fearing that she would have to leave the only man she had ever known as a father, she sobbed, "Oh Daddy, I don't want to go."

Robert Mays reassured the child that he would not let anyone take her away. But the Twiggs wanted a relationship with the child. Kimberly visited the brothers and sisters she had never met, but decided the situation had disrupted her life too much. As the years went on, she demanded that the Twiggs leave her alone.

Kimberly Mays hugs her grandmother in August 1993, after a judge allows her to stay in the custody of Robert Mays.

ADOLESCENT RIGHTS

At age fifteen, Kimberly was in a Sarasota, Florida, courtroom, asking a judge to break her connection to the Twiggs. "I want them out of my life and my life back," she tearfully testified.

In August 1993, the judge granted her wish. She no longer had to see her biological parents. Robert Mays would be her legal and "natural" father.

Kimberly Changes Her Mind Oddly, the story did not end there. In March 1994, Kimberly suddenly decided she did not want to live with Robert Mays anymore. She moved in with the Twiggs.

Robert had remarried again, and Kimberly was not happy with the arrangement. She also complained that her father was too strict about letting her go to parties and staying out late. At one point, she ran away and slept at a YMCA youth center. She told the other teenagers there that Robert felt she dated too many boys.

The two families got together to do what was best. Robert allowed Kimberly to stay with her biological parents while a judge decided the next move.

Many said that Kimberly was acting like a spoiled adolescent. But on May 14, 1994, Judge Stephen Dakan decided that Kimberly was entitled to make her own choices. He granted the Twiggs custody of the teen, and Robert Mays "reasonable visitation

The Rights of Homeless Children

Becoming homeless was bad enough for a woman in Putnam County, Illinois. But when school officials refused to continue educating her four children, she said, "I felt very frustrated, very angry, and very helpless."

Her supporters claimed she was being punished because she couldn't afford to pay taxes for school costs. They pointed out that when the woman had been living in an apartment, her children had been able to remain in school. Did that mean that the right to an education only applied to children when they weren't homeless? With at least 450,000 homeless children in the United States, people feared that other districts would follow Putnam County's lead.

This seemed particularly frightening since the population of homeless children was—and is—growing. In 1993, 30 percent of the people entering homeless shelters were children, up from 25 percent in 1989. For these youngsters, school serves an essential need.

"After children lose their home, the next security blanket for them to lose is usually their school and all their friends, and then they turn around and there's nothing much more that's left to lose," said Mary Balma, who has helped people in north central Illinois find housing.

Although all children are guaranteed an education under federal law, up to 33 percent of the country's homeless youth miss classes on a regular basis. This may have to do with family problems related to homelessness or the reluctance of local schools to admit the youngsters.

If these young people do not acquire adequate education and job skills, the chances are great that they will repeat the pattern of their parents. "Whether a homeless child receives an education . . . plays a big part in determining whether he or she becomes a homeless adult," said Sister Rose Marie Lorentzen, director of an Illinois shelter.

---

privileges." If any other difficulties arose, the families would have to settle the problems.

Despite the complicated nature of the Kimberly Mays case, there was a simple concern at the root of it. Even though Kimberly's behavior was not perfect, she was an individual with feelings, opinions, and rights. The judge's ruling confirmed that this teenager—and not the adults fighting for her—had the right to determine her own future.

3

Children's Rights in School

An adolescent may often feel trapped between two life phases. Not quite an adult, but not a little kid anymore either. For many adolescents, when older people try to discipline them, they may push back, expressing themselves through their choices of books, clothing, music, and speech.

On many occasions, school becomes the battleground for adolescents trying to declare their individuality.

Dress Codes

In the 1950s, schools all over America had dress codes. Girls were expected to wear conservative-looking skirts and blouses, while boys came to class in plain slacks and shirts.

Security was tightened at this Brooklyn, New York, high school after two students were shot in March 1992. Here, a student has his belongings checked with a metal detector.

Many administrators believed that, if students dressed conservatively, they would be well behaved and not question teachers' opinions.

This changed in the 1960s. Students began speaking out about the war in Vietnam. Soon, they were also debating other topics. Boys said they wanted to wear their hair long, and girls demanded the right to come to school in pants. The pupils wanted clothes that expressed their personalities and kept up with the fashions of the times.

One of the easiest ways to get a message across is to wear it on a T-shirt. But some schools believe that certain messages are not appropriate for the classroom.

In 1992, two brothers in South Hadley, Massachusetts, came to school in T-shirts that disturbed the administrators. Jeffrey Pyle, a high school senior, wore a shirt with an obscene message directed at people who drink and drive. Jonathan, a sophomore, had a shirt advertising an imaginary singing group called the "Coed Naked Band."

Although Jeffrey's shirt dealt with an important issue for young people, school administrators banned both T-shirts, claiming that the method of communication was "vulgar" and that the sexual nature of the slogans degraded women.

The boys' father took the school to court. He insisted that administrators had violated his sons' freedom of expression. A judge ruled in favor of the school, claiming officials had the right to create an atmosphere they believed was proper for education.

Other judges have also backed schools prohibiting pupils from expressing themselves in the following ways—dressing as the opposite sex at the prom; wearing T-shirts with drawings of drunk administrators; displaying earrings signifying allegiance to a street gang.

Clothes and Crime Around the United States, fears about gang and criminal activities have caused many administrators to examine what students wear to school. In some cases, it seemed that expensive items increased the potential for robbery. A student in Detroit was shot for his $135 down jacket. In Chicago, young people with colorful jackets displaying the names of sports teams were murdered.

Joe Clark, an African-American principal known nationally for his strict discipline policy, recommended that officials everywhere enforce dress codes. Clark—whose story was portrayed in the movie *Lean On Me*—said that when he eliminated expensive clothing from Eastside High School in Paterson, New Jersey, behavior improved. Instead of thinking about what to wear to school each day, he claimed, students concentrated on their studies.

Malcolm X fashions, shown here, have caused controversy because the African-American leader condoned the use of violence in the movement to achieve civil rights.

When everyone was required to wear the same outfits, he said that school violence and theft decreased.

Still, many students believe their fashion choices are misunderstood. When African-American youngsters in Thomasville, Georgia, shaved an X—in memory of the late African-American leader Malcolm X—into their hair, they were told to stop immediately. The students claimed that they were simply celebrating their heritage. And the local chapter of the NAACP, a national civil rights group, backed them up.

War over Music Just as young people try to make a statement with clothing in school, they seek out music they believe "speaks to them." Since the early days of popular music, school administrators, parents, and other adults have frequently objected to the music choices. Whether the sound was jazz in the 1920s, rock 'n' roll in the 1950s and 1960s, disco in the 1970s, punk rock in the 1980s, or rap in the 1990s, older people insisted the songs had a negative influence on teens.

Several years before her husband became vice president of the United States, Mary Elizabeth

30   ISSUES OF OUR TIME

(Tipper) Gore picked up one of her eleven-year-old daughter's record albums and was shocked by what she heard. Every song, it seemed, was about sex.

Gore began investigating further and found many songs promote drug use, sex, violence, suicide, and satanism. She worried that the music would encourage youngsters to experience the real thing.

In 1985, she formed the Parents Music Resource Center, which was dedicated to monitoring music directed at young people. She also signed an agreement with fifteen other spouses of senators and congressional representatives, pledging to put pressure on record companies and radio stations to play more wholesome music.

Tipper Gore led a fight to add warning labels to music that might be found offensive.

When Senate hearings were held on the issue, many in the music industry worried that they would soon be censored. Eventually, the Recording Industry Association of America agreed to place a special warning label on certain albums. But many albums continued to be released without the labels.

This controversy has persisted. Some politicians have demanded that laws be passed banning the sale of certain albums to teenagers. Anyone ignoring this restriction, they added, should be jailed.

Opponents of such proposals claimed the government would be acting like a bully, threatening to punish people for not sharing certain values. While teenagers continue to demand the right to listen to whatever they want, their defenders contend that some people are to quick to blame all of society's problems on rap, punk, and rock.

"There have been a number of studies of rock lyrics," said Roger Desmond, a psychologist at Connecticut's University of Bridgeport specializing in subjects involving adolescents and the media. "And they haven't been able to find any negative effects at all. In one study, it was found that if you ask high school students to tell you the story of their favorite song, they can't. What they're listening to is the beat."

Book Banning Some people feel that what children read has a greater impact on them than what they hear. In 1987, a group of Alabama parents became alarmed by textbooks they claimed encouraged "secular humanism," attitudes contrary to some religious teachings. One of the targeted publications was *Today's Teen,* a home economics textbook that included the following passage:

In March 1987, John Tyson, Jr., on behalf of Alabama's state department of education, asked the state to appeal Judge Hand's decision to ban forty-five books from the classroom.

"When you were very young, you probably accepted all your family's values without question. As people grow, see more of life, and learn to think on their own, they may choose other values. . . . Someday you may be faced with putting your ideals before theirs. Only you can judge your own values."

The parents specifically objected that the book encouraged young students to question lessons taught in the home. Judge Brevard Hand agreed, ordering *Today's Teen* and forty-four other books removed from a list of textbooks approved for Alabama students.

Eventually, a higher court set aside the judge's decision. But free-speech supporters argued that the damage had been done. Now, religious and other special interest groups in other states might move to have the same books banned. And some textbook publishers would be hesitant to distribute publications these organizations would not buy.

Searching Students School search policies have also caused a great deal of debate. When administrators look in pupils' lockers, young people feel that their privacy is being invaded. But officials claim that sometimes searches are the only way to keep order.

Tales of these incidents are endless. In upstate New York, teachers strip-searched an entire class of fifth graders to find three dollars one child reported missing. In Highland, Indiana, 2,800 junior high and high school students were forced to stay in their classrooms for three hours while specially trained dogs sniffed for drugs. In New Ipswich, New Hampshire, a principal and police chief installed a video camera in the boys' bathroom to find out which students were dealing drugs and vandalizing school property.

How legal are these actions? The case often used as a measuring stick took place at Piscataway High School in New Jersey. After a teacher found a fourteen-year-old freshman and her friend smoking cigarettes, the assistant vice principal ordered the freshman to hand over her purse. Inside, the administrator found a pack of cigarettes, marijuana, paper used to roll marijuana cigarettes, a clump of dollar bills, and a list of students who owed money to the teenager.

The girl was suspended for ten days; she took the school to court. The New Jersey Supreme Court ruled that the administrator had violated the freshman's rights under the Fourth Amendment, which forbids unlawful search and seizure.

The school appealed. In 1985, the U.S. Supreme Court decided the school had acted properly. Justice Byron White wrote of the "substantial need of teachers and administrators to maintain order in the schools." Schools could

Justice Byron White supported the right of a school to be able to conduct a search if the school felt it was necessary.

ADOLESCENT RIGHTS 35

search students, he said, if there were "reasonable grounds for suspecting that the search will turn up evidence that the student has violated or is violating either the law or the rules of the school." He added, however, that a mere "hunch" of something wrong was not enough.

Cases in which judges have ruled against administrators include searches of *every* student in a school when marijuana smoke has been smelled in a hallway, when walls have been defaced by graffiti, and when some students violated school rules by having personal radios.

As a rule, judges have allowed administrators to use trained dogs to sniff lockers for drugs. Strip searches, however, are frowned upon by judges. Said one, "It doesn't take a constitutional scholar to conclude that a nude search of a thirteen-year-old child is an invasion of constitutional rights. . . . More than that, it is a violation of any known principle of human decency."

Corporal Punishment Many children's advocates consider corporal punishment—hitting as a means of discipline—just as humiliating as strip searches. Although the practice has grown less common in recent years, teachers and administrators in many localities still strike pupils.

Can A School Intervene in Your Social Life?

Prom night is supposed to be one of the highlights of high school. But that special event was tarnished in Wedowee, Alabama, in 1994, in an uproar over a principal's refusal to allow interracial dating.

Although the original issue was one of race, it sparked a larger question. Young people everywhere asked what gave an adult, who was not the parent of the kids involved, the right to approve or reject their choice of dates. Teenagers and adults were outraged at the infringement of children's rights.

ReVonda Bowen and her boyfriend, Chris Brown, at Randolph County High School.

Hulond Humphries, a white man, had been principal of Randolph County High School for twenty-five years. When he learned that at least a dozen interracial couples were planning to attend the prom, he became alarmed by what seemed to be an increasing trend of interracial dating and canceled the event. He claimed that there was already tension between African-Americans and whites in the school, and someone might get hurt if interracial dating were permitted.

When he expressed his views to some of his 680 students, he was challenged by ReVonda Bowen, the sixteen-year-old junior-class president. ReVonda, who planned to attend the prom with her white boyfriend, mentioned that her mother was African-American and her father white. The principal told the girl that her parents had made a "mistake" by having an interracial child.

He was suspended after making the comment, but later reinstated. Still, the prom went on and interracial couples attended. But the controversy did not die. African-American students and white supporters boycotted classes for several days. And ReVonda Bowen filed a civil rights lawsuit against her principal.

In 1977, in the *Ingraham v. Wright* case, the Supreme Court ruled that corporal punishment was not "cruel and unusual punishment," as its opponents claimed. But that ruling did not silence the debate. In Florida, for example, hitting is still permitted, but the state has warned against "excessive corporal punishment." This has left everyone wondering where acceptable discipline ends and child abuse begins.

In the late 1980s, more and more schools discontinued the practice of corporal punishment. By 1991, it had been banned in public schools in twenty-two states; only nine states forbade it six years earlier. During the same period, polls showed an 11 percent drop in the number of parents who said they spanked their children at home.

Nonetheless, a sizable number of Americans still believe that authorities have become too lenient with children. Although many people were outraged when Michael Fay, an eighteen-year-old from Ohio, was lashed with a cane in Singapore in 1994 after being convicted of spray-painting graffiti on cars, some politicians and citizens urged the same punishment in the United States.

At the time that the Fay "caning" case was in the headlines, politicians all over America proposed similar measures. A California legislative committee urged spanking young graffiti writers in court. Offenders under eighteen years of age would have their clothed buttocks whacked with a wooden paddle. Either a parent or a court officer would deliver the beating. And in Cincinnati, Ohio, a city councilman recommended "public paddling" for vandalism.

One case that sparked discussions over corporal punishment was Michael Fay's, an American teen who was physically punished while in Singapore.

A large percentage of the people who favor these steps also approve of corporal punishment in the classroom. But Ann Cohn Donnelly, of the National Committee for Prevention of Child Abuse, has contended that beating is not the answer.

"Teachers have alternatives," she told the magazine *U.S. News and World Report*. "Sometimes a child needs to be separated from the situation. Remember the image of sitting in the corner or being removed from class. Sometimes things can be talked through. Always, what is important is to help the child understand why what he or she did was wrong. Hitting a child with a board may correct behavior for a short time, but it doesn't tell you why the child behaved that way."

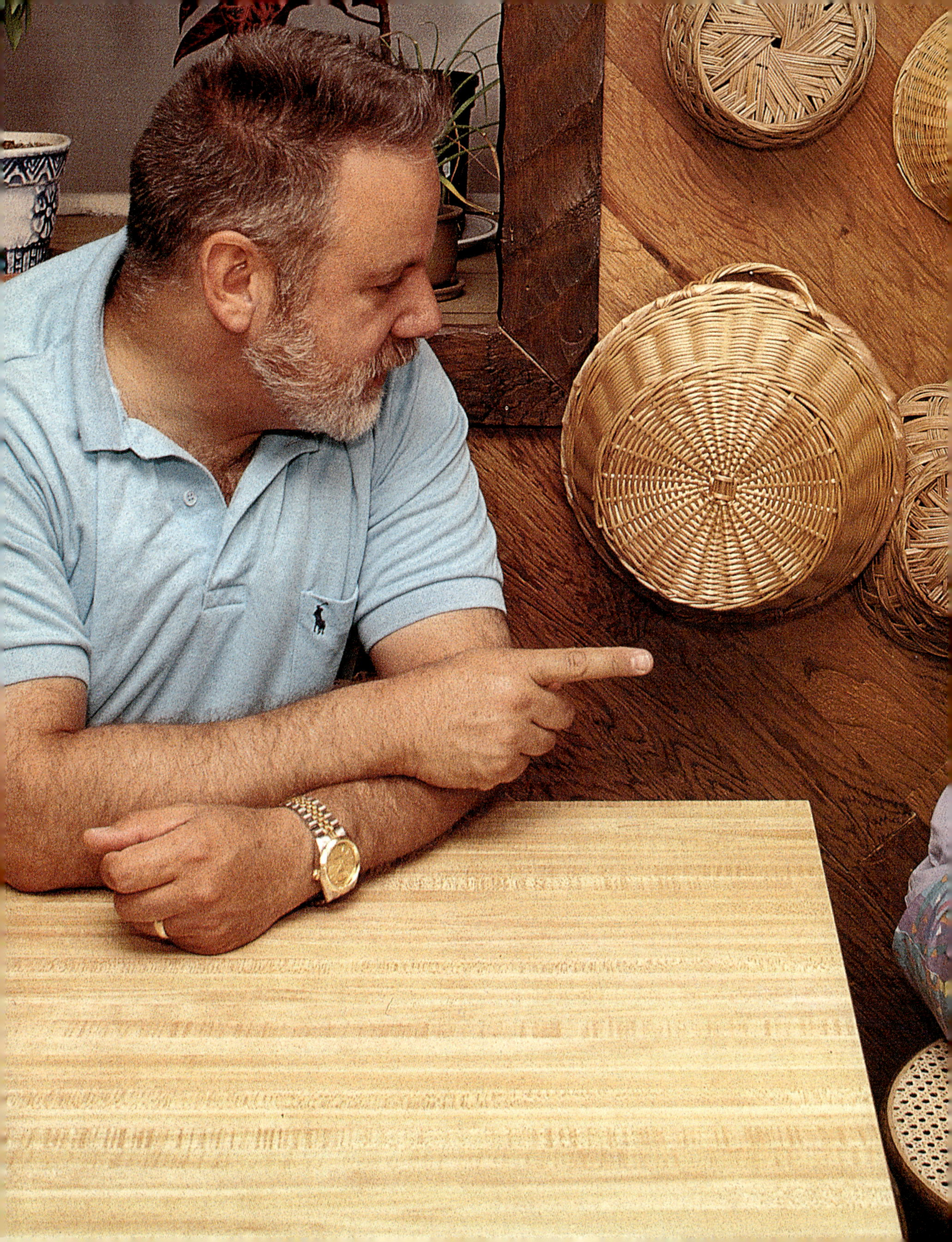

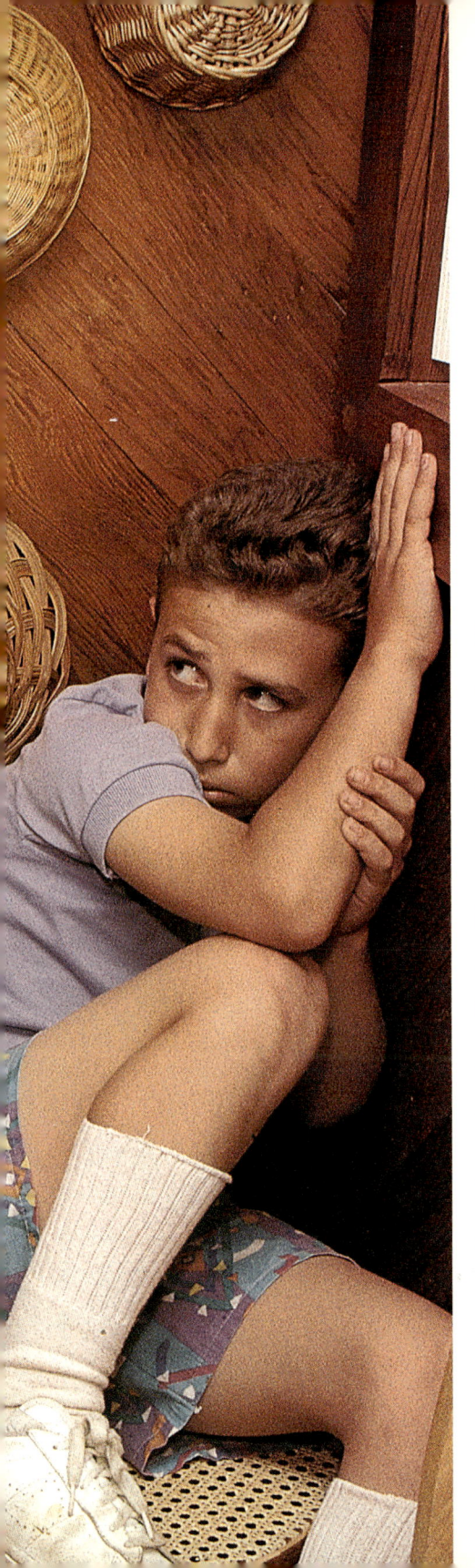

4

Problems at Home

Child abuse has always been a problem. But in the last few years, it has become a plague. In 1993, there were 1 million confirmed cases of child abuse and neglect in the United States, and 1,300 youngsters died as a result.

Could this have been prevented? Many believe that it could have. Of the 1,300 murdered children, 42 percent had previously been brought to the attention of child protection agencies, but had not been removed from the abusive situations.

Richard Gelles, director of the University of Rhode Island's Family Violence Research Program, has complained, "The child welfare system stands over the bodies, shows you pictures of the caskets, and still does things to keep kids at risk."

Most young people rely on their parents to help protect their rights. But growing rates of child abuse in America has made this a more complicated issue.

Should Troubled Families Stay Together?

The child protection system is supposed to shield children from violence, but critics say its real aim is to keep families together at any cost. The policy they criticize came about because of another form of injustice. In the 1960s and 1970s, many children were taken away from poor African-American parents, because the system decided those parents were unable to care for their children. A new law was needed to protect families from discrimination, even if there were problems in the household.

In 1980, the Adoption Assistance and Child Welfare Act was passed. This federal law stated that

Social service workers receive training on parent rehabilitation and counseling for abuse or neglect cases.

parents who could not care for their children had eighteen months to straighten out their lives. If the parents were drug addicts, they could use that time to go through rehabilitation, while their children were in foster care. Then, the family would be reunited.

Some say this approach has been taken to an unreasonable extreme—and one that leaves children in danger. Even when parents have a record of abusing their children physically or sexually, the goal is to keep the family together. "We've oversold the fact that all families can be saved," said Marcia Robinson Lowry, children's rights specialist for the American Civil Liberties Union. "All families *can't* be saved."

Foster Care Troubles

On the other side of the issue are people who point out flaws in the foster care system. Douglas Besharov, a director of the National Center of Child Abuse and Neglect, said that more children are mistreated in foster homes or institutions than by their natural families.

One example is Matthew, a California boy who was removed from his home after social workers suspected his parents of child abuse. When Matthew was accused of stealing baseball cards from his foster parents' grandson, he said he was forced to strip in front of the entire family. At other times, he claimed, he was spanked with a wooden paddle and locked in a dark bathroom for the night.

Why would a foster family take a child into their home and then abuse him? Sadly, some foster parents get involved simply because the government pays them for each child they shelter. Despite the money Matthew's foster parents received, the boy said he was fed mainly soup, and he felt hungry most of the time.

Children who have been through the foster care system frequently become distrustful of it. Although parents who cast minors out of their homes without support may be guilty of neglect, the children tend not to alert the authorities. In some cases, the youngsters would rather try their luck on the streets than in a foster home.

Investigating Abuse Through the years, the government has tried to pass laws safeguarding children in all types of living situations. Since 1974, professionals who observe children—from teachers to social workers—have been responsible for reporting suspected abuse. Anyone neglecting to do so can face criminal charges.

Still, many cases of child abuse are overlooked. This is often because caseworkers, who are in charge of evaluating the circumstances of troubled families, are overworked. In New York City, for instance, some of these workers are involved with forty cases at a time and simply cannot devote the proper attention to any.

Also, many social workers do not have specific, extensive training in abuse issues. Their job is to *help* families in need, not to play the role of a detective investigating abuse. Said West Virginia social worker Leroy Schultz, "We are being thrust into a situation that we are not prepared for."

Many times, abuse remains a mystery unless the young victims speak out. Often, abused children

A caseworker investigates a child abuse case in New York City.

keep quiet, fearing greater punishment from their abusers. But many children have escaped bad circumstances because they told a teacher, friend, guidance counselor, police officer, or member of the clergy about their plight. Many of these people are required by law to help, but they cannot assist if they do not know about the situation.

Custody Combat

Even in homes where there has never been abuse, children's lives can be turned upside down when parents divorce. Sometimes, the husband and wife reach an agreement about where the children will live without going to court. But in many instances, Americans are engaging in custody battles.

During different periods of history, courts would favor different parents. "Until the middle of the nineteenth century, fathers had an absolute right to custody," said Mary Ann Mason, author of the book *From Father's Property to Children's Rights: The History of Child Custody in the United States*. "It was because children were an important part of the labor force in homes and on farms." But that changed as greater numbers of women demanded equal rights. By the twentieth century, mothers usually were awarded custody.

One of the demands of the women's rights movement over the past twenty-five years has been that fathers take a greater role in raising children. As this change occurred, men who became committed to actively raising their children were reluctant to give up custody in a divorce. Since the late 1970s, courts have begun looking at mothers and fathers as being equally equipped to raise children.

But the information presented in court is frequently incomplete. In some cases, psychologists and social workers interview family members over the telephone rather than visiting the home and seeing how the family lives. Sometimes, only a small portion of the whole story is offered in the courtroom. This creates confusion for a judge trying to decide what is best for the children.

Sometimes, parents get so involved in fighting for custody that the children feel ignored. This may cause children to take desperate steps to get attention. They might misbehave or threaten to move to the rival parent's home just to see if the parent currently in custody really cares.

Many times, the controversy distracts the child from schoolwork. One father remembered how his daughter began slipping behind in class. "There were problems," he said, "lack of concentration, she wasn't listening. She developed terrible headaches. She feels like a yo-yo."

When a child expresses a desire to live with a particular parent, courts may ignore the request.

Even when a judge accommodates the young person's wish, the child might feel guilty later about leaving one parent for the other.

So who should decide custody? The answer is often unclear. A child may prefer one parent to another. But sometimes that could be for the wrong reasons: A "fun" mother who does not care if her child attends school can harm the youngster more than a strict father who is devoted to education. Yet, the child's wishes must be considered. The young person's opinion is no less valid than that of a parent—who may be battling for custody for selfish reasons—or a social worker who does not know the full story.

Teenage Abortion

Few issues stir emotions more than the right of a teenage girl to have an abortion without a parent's consent.

In 1988, Becky Bell, a seventeen-year-old Indiana girl, discovered that she was pregnant. She believed her parents would be hurt by this news, so she kept it a secret from them. She would get an abortion, she reasoned, and her parents would never have to find out. But when Becky went to the clinic, she was told that Indiana law required her to get her parents' permission before the procedure could be performed.

Becky thought about driving south to Kentucky, where parental consent was not required to have an abortion. In the end, though, she decided to go to an illegal clinic in Indianapolis. However, something went wrong during the abortion. When Becky returned home, her lungs filled with fluid and she started to hemorrhage. Tragically, a short time later, she died.

"Becky didn't want to hurt us," her mother Karen stated. "The thing is, this has ended up breaking our hearts."

Every year, more than one million American teenagers become pregnant and about half choose to have an abortion. In 1976, the Supreme Court ruled that it was up to individual states to decide if minors had to inform their parents first. If so, there is a provision for girls who believe they would be in danger if they told their parents. They can appeal privately to a judge. This method is known as "judicial bypass."

Members of the Right to Life movement, which is opposed to abortion for any reason, insist on greater restrictions. Parents should give their children moral guidance, they say, and teenagers are just too young to make a decision about something as serious as abortion.

"Thousands of unborn children are murdered each year by teenagers who aren't mature enough to

A group of young people participates in a 1991 Pro-Choice demonstration, exercising their right to voice their opinion.

know what they're doing," said John Paul Wauk, a member of the Right to Life movement.

The Pro-Choice movement, which supports a female's right to decide whether she wants an abortion, counters that parental consent laws violate a girl's right to privacy and endanger her by denying quick medical attention.

50   ISSUES OF OUR TIME

Do Kids Have the Right to Refuse Medical Treatment?

The doctors had bad news for Billy Best. The youngster had Hodgkin's disease, a form of cancer. With proper treatment the ailment could be cured, but the process would be very painful and take a long time.

Billy tried the treatments. After several months, he wondered whether the agony was worthwhile. Finally, in 1994, the sixteen-year-old ran away from home. "The reason I left," he explained in a note to his parents, "is because I could not stand going to the hospital every week. I feel like the medicine is killing me instead of helping me."

Billy did return home, but his case brought up many questions. Do young people have the right to refuse medical treatment? May parents or doctors force teenagers to go to the hospital? Should a critically ill youngster be allowed to choose his or her own death?

This was the decision made by Benito Agrelo, a fifteen-year-old from Coral Springs, Florida. After two liver transplants, Benito stopped taking his medication, and experienced painful side effects. In June 1994, the Florida Department of Health and Rehabilitative Services ordered that the teenager be removed from his parents' home and placed in a hospital for treatment. But a judge overruled the decree, insisting the boy had the right to make choices about his own life. Two months later, the youngster died at home.

The rules about this issue are unclear. In most states, a doctor must determine whether a teenager—usually at least fourteen years old—understands the advantages, dangers, and alternatives regarding treatment. If so, the child is considered a "mature minor" and can receive care without the approval of parents. However, there are no laws about a teenager's decision to *reject* treatment.

Young people argue that they—not parents or doctors—should be the only ones involved in the final choice. Some adults counter that teenagers are not mature enough to be given that responsibility.

"It comes down to communication between the teenager, parent, and health care provider," Dr. Arthur Elster of the American Medical Association told the *New York Times*. "If we understand and respect the teenager, other things will fall into place. That doesn't mean there won't be problems, but we'll be able to manage them better."

Support groups are among the best places families can seek advice. Groups for teenagers with cancer include: Chemocare, 231 North Avenue West, Westfield, NJ 07090, (908) 233-1103 in New Jersey, and (800) 55-CHEMO in other states; American Cancer Society, 1599 Clifton Road N.E., Atlanta, GA 30329, (800) ACS-2345; National Cancer Institute information service, (800) 4-CANCER.

This was the position taken by Becky Bell's father, Bill, after her death. "My daughter was denied the right to make a safe and reasonable choice on her own," he said.

ADOLESCENT RIGHTS

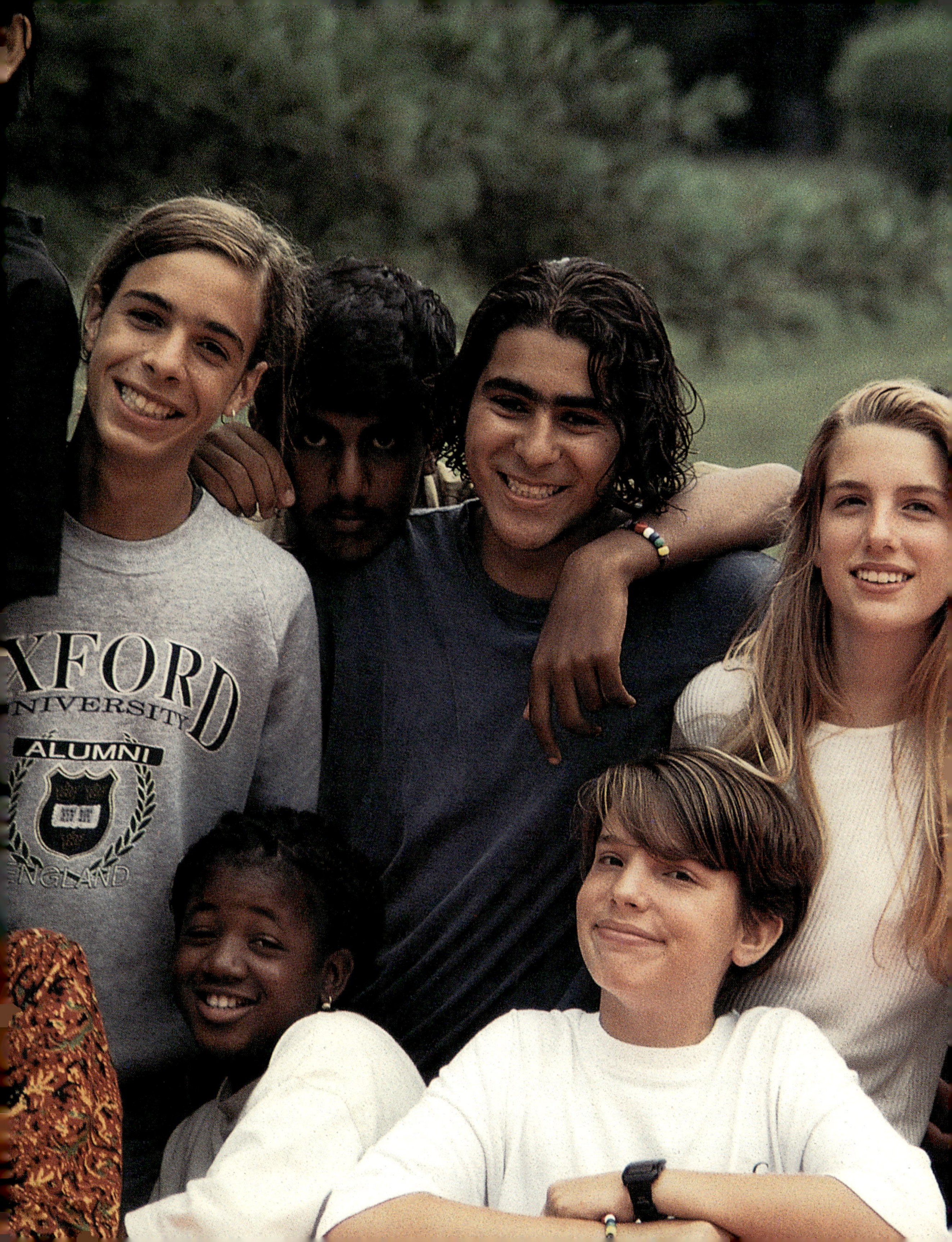
XFORD
ALUMNI
ENGLAND

5

Looking Ahead

With Americans everywhere calling for stricter methods to combat crime, teenagers who get into trouble with the law can expect harsher treatment than in the past. The issue of protected rights for all children, however, is not getting lost in the fight to reduce teen crime.

A Movement on the Rise The larger issue of *all* children's rights is being given increased attention. The children's rights movement has continued to expand in recent years. As the United Nations (UN) formulates an international policy for the treatment of children, the National Education Association (NEA) has published its own

This international group of young people gathered at the Heart's Bend World Children's Center in Vermont to learn about securing the rights of children worldwide.

Children's Bill of Rights. The document says that every American child is entitled to proper nutrition, medical care, quality education, a secure place to live, and freedom from abuse, violence, and discrimination.

Harvard Law School professor Martha Minow explained that children need special laws to understand that they live in a community "with others who care about them." In an article she wrote in the *Los Angeles Times*, she said that children must know that society will protect them if their parents or other adults wish to do harm.

"My responsibilities to my child include living under a system of laws guaranteeing the youngster's safety," Minow said. "If I fail her, the society—through laws and customs—will step in."

In 1992, several groups from around the nation banded together to form the National Coalition for Youth. The organization launched a ten-year-long program aimed at young people in thirty cities. Goals include changing laws, improving services, and making more people aware of the many problems children face.

"We're doing a brutal disservice to America's children," said co-chair John Ramsey. "We need to change our ways." He advised adults to "make that long-term commitment to making a healthier society." Correcting health care, education, and housing

Children of the Earth: A Worldwide Movement

In September 1990, the world's leaders gathered at the United Nations to address the needs of children. It was the largest meeting of this kind that has ever taken place. These leaders agreed to produce plans of action for the development and needs of children, as well as to support the Convention on the Rights of the Child, a Bill of Rights for children. One of the main points of the Convention is to allow youngsters to participate in creating their own future.

In 1970, Nina Meyerhof started Heart's Bend Camp, a 100-acre camp in Vermont, running summer programs oriented toward developing community projects, and nurturing multicultural cooperation. Twenty years later, at the same time as the 1990 UN meeting, children from twenty-two countries met at the Heart's Bend World Children's Center to discuss their own plans for a bright future. At the 1990 summer meeting, participants wrote a document called "A Children's Declaration of Peace" and participated in creating a new forum for themselves called Children of the Earth.

Since that time, Children of the Earth has brought together kids from around the world to teach them how to create and implement their own plans for the future. In 1991, Children of the Earth hosted an international conference for young leaders, during which children from twenty-five countries met with UN officials, UNICEF representatives, and representatives from the U.S. Mission to the UN to discuss their concerns.

In 1992, the Coalition for Children of the Earth held a conference in Switzerland that included children from thirty-three countries. These participants made a presentation to a board of international human rights experts. And in 1993, at the same time and place as the UN World Conference of Human Rights, a conference of 175 kids from 40 countries met. These young adults, many of whom were from conflicting regions such as Bosnia and Serbia, and Israel and Palestine, dealt with one another with remarkable harmony. Two of them were selected to address the UN officials—the first time in history that children representing children worldwide have ever addressed world leaders.

"We children feel that our human rights have been violated," Sleepy Eye La Fromboise, a Native American from New York State, told UN representatives. "We feel that it is vital that we are part of the decisions that affect us. We need to be recognized and heard. If the children can continue to be united and are given a chance within the United Nations, generation after generation, then there can be peace on earth."

Today, the Coalition for Children of the Earth is preparing for the 1995 World Summit of Children. This summit will consist of many simultaneous meetings of children around the world interacting through telecommunications technologies. The major goal of the 1995 summit is to create a proposal for a young general assembly to become an official part of the United Nations. Children of the Earth is dedicated to educating children of their rights and responsibilities as global citizens and empowering them to make a difference in both their present and future.

for youth, he said, would "help produce a shift in values and attitudes toward one that favors and better cares for children."

A City Commits Itself to Youth
In San Francisco, California, that attitude has been translated into law. In 1991, due largely to a campaign by an association called Coleman Advocates for Children and Youth, voters approved a special "children's amendment." This made San Francisco the first U.S. city to set aside money from property taxes for a "children's fund."

The first year, 1.5 percent of all the property taxes—$6 million—went into the fund. The plan is for 2.5 percent of property taxes to be contributed annually over the next nine years. In 1993, the city spent $13 million on enriching the lives of children through tutoring, job training, and other programs. Now, a child who may have ended up living in poverty or getting into trouble has a better chance at becoming a successful adult.

Tougher Laws
Between October 1990 and June 1991, Florida authorities determined that 3,248 children who were under the age of eighteen should be tried as adults for violations that ranged from alcohol possession to murder.

Colorado saw tough measures introduced in 1993, after a fourteen- and fifteen-year-old—both students at a suburban middle school—stole a car and fatally shot the patrol officer who stopped them. Plans were made to put young offenders in military style "boot camps" to learn discipline. Graffiti and gang activity would be more severely punished. Schools were to stress "respect for authority," with officials given increased power to suspend and expel pupils. After thirty days, the number of students ejected from school was 50 percent higher than the number expelled during the same month in previous years.

Hillary Rodham Clinton's Involvement

There have been many positive breakthroughs in the fight to secure children's rights. First Lady Hillary Rodham Clinton has been a backer of what she has called "the healthy development of our youth" for years. Before her husband was elected president, Ms. Rodham Clinton, a lawyer, compared

Hillary Clinton has made the rights of children a priority in the Clinton administration.

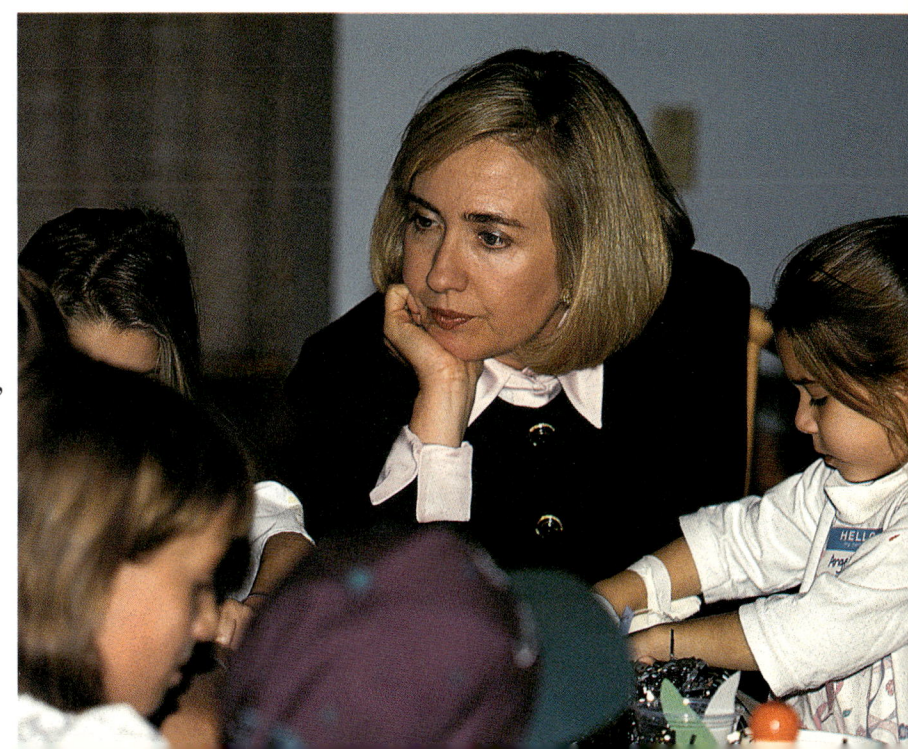

the children's rights movement to the civil rights movement. In the past, she said, it was believed that children were not capable of making decisions for themselves. This same logic, she added, was frequently used to discriminate against African-Americans and women. She expressed the desire to see all three groups free from bias.

During the 1992 presidential election, Bill Clinton's foes claimed that his wife's support of children's rights weakened the family. They were particularly outraged over her opinion that young people should be permitted to speak for themselves—rather than assuming that parents knew best. If everybody thought this way, Ms. Rodham Clinton's opponents contended, children would stop listening to their mothers and fathers.

But Lewis Pitts, a lawyer involved in arguing the case for Gregory Kingsley—the twelve-year-old who divorced his mother—insisted that Hillary Clinton's critics were overreacting. "The victory we won insures the right of the child to make important choices before his or her life is completely ruined," Pitts said.

In the magazine *The Nation*, Pitts emphasized his message by quoting Garbriela Mistral, a poet from Chile: "Many things we need can wait, the child cannot. . . . To him we cannot say tomorrow, his name is today."

The Children's Defense Fund

Children today face overwhelming obstacles. According to a report called *The State of America's Children 1991*, published by the Children's Defense Fund:

• Every 55 seconds an infant is born to a mother who is not a high school graduate.

• Every 32 seconds a 15- to 19-year-old woman becomes pregnant.

• Every 64 seconds an infant is born to a teenage mother.

Since 1973, the Children's Defense Fund has spoken out for children unable to vote or communicate directly with people in power. The group, which pays particular attention to poor, minority, and disabled youngsters, attempts to educate the country about children's problems, while reaching young people before they get sick, pregnant, drop out of school, clash with the law, or become homeless.

The founder, Marian Wright Edelman, is the daughter of a Baptist minister, who taught her that helping others is the "rent" one pays for living. "Service was as essential a part of my upbringing as eating and sleeping," she said.

The organization started when workers searched the country in an effort to find the two million children listed on census data as being out of school. The group found that public schools were often not helping young people who were poor, pregnant, minorities, disabled, or unable to speak English.

Over the years, the Children's Defense Fund has had an enormous impact. It has:

• worked to persuade Congress to pass the Education for All Handicapped Children Act in 1974;

• coordinated the efforts of 2,000 volunteers

Marian Wright Edelman, head of the Children's Defense Fund

and 32 national organizations in developing teen pregnancy prevention programs; and

• supported City Lights, a Washington, D.C., school for children dismissed as "unteachable" or "untreatable."

Edelman is now considered one of America's most influential leaders and has been consulted by the Clinton administration on children's issues. First Lady Hillary Rodham Clinton is a longtime supporter of the organization. Edelman maintains that "real change" will come about only when every American gets involved.

"America will have to be changed by millions of people speaking up," she said, "changed from the bottom up, not the top down."

Glossary

caseworker A social service employee who works to help troubled families and individuals.

child advocate An individual committed to children's rights.

corporal punishment Physical punishment that involves striking the body with hands or an object, such as spanking or paddling.

foster parent An adult who temporarily provides a home and care for a child, often receiving financial assistance from the state for doing so.

juvenile court A special court that handles cases for young people, who are usually under the age of eighteen.

natural parent A biological, or birth, parent.

Pro-Choice Belief in a woman's right to choose to have an abortion.

Right to Life A movement opposed to a woman's right to choose to have an abortion.

secular humanism A term used by some religious groups to describe a philosophy rejecting God.

U.S. Supreme Court The nation's highest court, which has the authority to rule on the constitutionality of laws.

For Further Reading

Berry, Joy. *Every Kid's Guide to Laws That Relate to Kids in the Community.* Chicago, IL: Childrens Press, 1987.

_____. *Every Kid's Guide to the Juvenile Justice System.* Chicago, IL: Childrens Press, 1987.

Greenberg, Keith. *Out of the Gang.* Minneapolis: Lerner, 1992.

Hjelmeland, Andy. *Kids in Jail.* Minneapolis: Lerner, 1992.

O'Connor, Karen. *Homeless Children.* San Diego: Lucent Books, 1989.

Otfinoski, Steve. *Marian Wright Edelman: Defender of Children's Rights.* Woodbridge, CT: Blackbirch Press, 1992.

Terkel, Susan, *Understanding Child Custody.* New York: Franklin Watts, 1991.

Source Notes

Arnold, Michael S. "Crowding, Violence Plague Youth Detention Centers." The *Washington Post*, September 14, 1993.

"Black Students Complain of Georgia School Dress Code." *Jet*, October 18, 1993.

Cohn, Bob. "From Chattel to Full Citizens." *Newsweek*, September 21, 1992.

Conover, Kirsten. "Child Advocacy Groups Form Coalition." *Christian Science Monitor*, February 12, 1992.

Eisenman, Russell. "Society Confronts the Hard-Core Youthful Offender." *USA Today*, January 1994.

Hardy, James Earl. "X-Rated Rock and Roll." *Scholastic Update*, May 18, 1990.

Ingrassia, Michele, and John McCormack. "Why Leave Children with Bad Parents?" *Newsweek*, April 25, 1994.

Jacobbi, Marianne. "Whose Little Girl Is Kimberly?" *Good Housekeeping*, March 1989.

Kasindorf, Jeanie Russell. "Degrees of Separation." *New York*, February 28, 1994.

Kotlowitz, Alex. "Their Crimes Don't Make Them Adults." *New York Times Magazine*, February 13, 1994.

Rolin, David Oliver. "Old Enough to Choose?" *Scholastic Update*, April 20, 1990.

Simpson, Michael. "Looking for Trouble." *NEA Today*, October 1992.

Stevens, Peter, and Marian Cide. "The First Chapter of Children's Rights." *American Heritage*, July/August 1990.

Tippet, Sarah. "I've Got the Family I Always Wanted." *Ladies Home Journal*, April 1993.

Zegart, Dan. "Solomon's Choice." *Ms.*, June 1989.

Zirkel, Perry A. "You Bruise, You Lose." *Phi Delta Kappah*, January 1990.

Index

Adoption Assistance and Welfare Act, 42–43
Agrelo, Benito, 51
American Society for the Prevention of Cruelty to Animals, 7

Balma, Mary, 25
Beaumont Learning Center, 13
Bell, Becky, 48–49, 51
Bell, Bill, 51
Bergh, Henry, 7
Best, Billy, 51
Besharov, Douglas, 43
Bowen, ReVonda, 37
Bush, George, 8

Carey, Jane, 19–20
Child abuse, 6, 10, 38, 41
Children of the Earth, 55
Children's Defense Fund, 59
Children's rights
    abortion and, 48–51
    advocates for, 5, 12, 32, 36
    book banning and, 32–34
    child abuse and, 41
    corporal punishment and, 36–39
    crime and, 9–13
    custody battles and, 46–48
    dress codes and, 27–30
    foster care and, 43–44
    homelessness and, 25
    laws and, 7–9, 56–57
    medical treatment and, 51
    music and, 30–32
    school searches and, 34–36

Clark, Joe, 29–30
Clinton, Bill, 8, 58
Clinton, Hillary Rodham, 57–58, 59
Coleman Advocates for Children and Youth, 56
Congress, 7, 8, 9, 59
Convention on the Rights of the Child, 8, 55

Dakan, Stephen, 24
Department of Justice, 10
Desmond, Roger, 32
Donnelly, Ann Cohn, 39

Edelman, Marian Wright, 59
Elster, Arthur, 51

Family Violence Research Program, 41
Fay, Michael, 38

Gelles, Richard, 41
Gerry, Elbridge, 7
Gore, Mary Elizabeth (Tipper), 30–31

Hand, Brevard, 34
Hardee Memorial Hospital, 20, 22
Heart's Bend Camp, 55
Humphries, Hulond, 37

Ingraham v. Wright, 37

Juvenile detention facility, 12, 13

Kingsley, Gregory, 5, 15–19, 20, 58
Kingsley, Rachel, 15, 16, 18–19

Kingsley, Ralph, 16
Kirk, Thomas S., 19

LaFromboise, Sleepy Eye, 55
Lake County Boys Ranch, 16, 17
Lean On Me, 29
Lorentzen, Sister Rose Marie, 25
Lowry, Marcia Robinson, 43

Mason, Mary Ann, 46
Mays, Barbara, 22
Mays, Kimberly, 22, 23–24
 case of, 20–25
Mays, Robert, 22, 23, 24
McCormack, Mary, 6, 7
McCormack, Mary Ellen, 6, 7
McCormack, Thomas, 6
Meyerhof, Nina, 8, 55
Minow, Martha, 54
Mistral, Garbriela, 58

National Center on Child Abuse and Neglect, 43
National Coalition for Youth, 54
National Committee for Prevention of Child Abuse, 39
National Education Association (NEA), 53
New York Society for the Prevention of Cruelty to Children, 7

Parents Music Resource Center, 31
Pitts, Lewis, 58
Pro-Choice movement, 50
Pyle, Jeffrey, 28
Pyle, Jonathan, 28

Ramsey, John, 54
Recording Industry Association of America, 31
Right to Life movement, 49–50
Russ, George, 16, 17, 18
Russ, Lizabeth, 15, 17
Russ, Shawn. *See* Gregory Kingsley.

Sanders, Bernie, 8
Schultz, Leroy, 45
Supreme Court, 7, 8, 9, 35, 37, 49
Sutton, Maxwell, 15

Twigg, Arlena Beatrice, 21, 22
Twigg, Ernest, 21
Twigg, Regina, 20, 21
Twigg, Vivia, 21

United Nations (UN), 53, 55

Vietnam War, 8, 9, 28

Wauk, John Paul, 50
Wheeler, Etta Angell, 6, 7
White, Byron, 35–36

Photo Credits
Cover: Blackbirch Graphics, Inc.; pp. 4, 10, 19, 21, 22, 26, 33: AP/Wide World Photos; p. 7: The George Sim Johnston Archives of The New York Society for the Prevention of Cruelty to Children; p. 11: ©Jon Levy/Gamma Liaison; p. 14: ©Tom Spitz/Orlando Sentinel/SABA; pp. 18, 20: ©Steve Starr/SABA; p. 23: ©Orlando Sentinel/Frank Rivera/Gamma Liaison; p. 30: ©Levy/Liaison USA; p. 31: ©Cynthia Johnson/Gamma Liaison; p. 35: Johnson/Liaison USA; p. 37: ©Karim Shamsa-Basha/Birmingham Post Herald/SABA; p. 39: ©Ralf Finn Hestoft/SABA; p. 40: ©PhotoEdit; pp. 42, 45: ©Yvonne Hemsey/Gamma Liaison; p. 50: Halebian/Liaison USA; p. 52: ©Tanya Stone, for Children of the Earth; p. 57: ©Najlah Feanny/SABA; p. 59: Westenberger/Liaison USA.